The Little Book of Speaking Up

The Little Book of
Speaking Up

Find Your Voice in
5 Minutes a Day
with 65 Whole-Body
Exercises

Jutta Ritschel

Illustrations by
Lena Ellermann

Translated by
Alta L. Price

THE EXPERIMENT

NEW YORK

The Little Book of Speaking Up: *Find Your Voice in 5 Minutes a Day*
Copyright © 2019 by Jutta Ritschel
Translation copyright © 2019 by Alta L. Price
Illustrations copyright © 2019 by Lena Ellermann

Originally published in German as *Einfach gut gestimmt!* by Bastei Lübbe in
2019. First published in North America by The Experiment, LLC, in 2019.

The Experiment, LLC
220 East 23rd Street, Suite 600, New York, NY 10010-4658
theexperimentpublishing.com

This book contains the opinions and ideas of its author. It is intended to
provide helpful and informative material on the subjects addressed in the book.
It is sold with the understanding that the author and publisher are not engaged in
rendering medical, health, or any other kind of personal professional services in the
book. The author and publisher specifically disclaim all responsibility for any liability, loss, or risk—personal or otherwise—that is incurred as a consequence, directly
or indirectly, of the use and application of any of the contents of this book.

THE EXPERIMENT and its colophon are registered trademarks of
The Experiment, LLC. Many of the designations used by manufacturers and sellers
to distinguish their products are claimed as trademarks. Where those designations
appear in this book and The Experiment was aware of a trademark claim, the designations have been capitalized.

The Experiment's books are available at special discounts when purchased in
bulk for premiums and sales promotions as well as for fund-raising or educational
use. For details, contact us at info@theexperimentpublishing.com.

Library of Congress Cataloging-in-Publication Data available upon request

ISBN 978-1-61519-606-7
Ebook ISBN 978-1-61519-607-4

Cover and text design by Beth Bugler | Cover illustration by Lena Ellermann

Manufactured in China

First printing September 2019
10 9 8 7 6 5 4 3 2 1

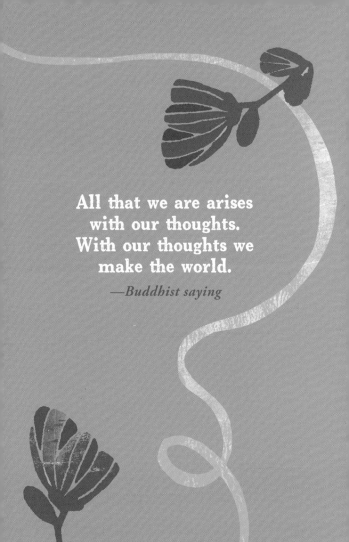

All that we are arises
with our thoughts.
With our thoughts we
make the world.

—*Buddhist saying*

Contents

Warming Up—Tuning In

My story

The voice is my life's work. Even as a little kid I loved singing, both with my mother and by myself. Later on, I sang in church, in my school choir, and while practicing the piano at home. Throughout my early years I came into contact with all sorts of vocal styles in my music studies and beyond. Some of my teachers tried to shape all of their students on a single vocal model, while others took a different approach, aiming to develop each student's personal voice as if it were a unique treasure. Eventually, I started studying to become a music teacher and chose to focus my thesis work on the development of breathing and vocal games for children. Despite my undeniably playful and joyful approach, my initial teaching focus was on vocal training.

Over the years I kept noticing how people who sing, regardless of age, have a certain glow about them and begin to shine from within. The connection between voice and harmony—in all senses of the word—became especially clear to me when a serious vocal injury suddenly wrenched me from my (perhaps overly) full life. At first my doctor prescribed silence; I hadn't voluntarily spoken for a while anyway, since every word hurt my throat. Singing had been my elixir of life, my beloved profession as a music teacher, even my everyday mode of communication—and suddenly it was forbidden. I couldn't talk on the phone and had to step back from my choir. I couldn't even yell up the stairs, so I resorted to clapping my hands to summon my kids to the dinner table. I was really taken aback to lose so many abilities. It was a frustrating, difficult time, and yet later revealed itself to be a deeply valuable experience. I "practiced silence" and dove into other creative activities, like writing, as I sought other means of expression. I had time to think, reflect, and read deeply on the subject: I devoured books and articles on breathing and the voice, holistic medicine, psychology, and psychosomatic phenomena. Mindfulness and meditation also came into my life because silence, in its own unique way, can lead us to the very core of our own personality. Beyond all those books, I explored different approaches to the voice, especially as it's studied in the field of speech therapy.

The next decisive development occurred during my three-year training to become a breath therapist. Breathing is an all-encompassing experience, and the path to more fully develop it is necessarily holistic. The more freely we allow our breath to flow, the freer we become—physically, mentally, and spiritually—and the more our own core selves can unfold. Free-flowing breath is the basis of a free voice and a harmonious personality. During my time of relative silence, my voice developed as never before. By the second year, once my voice had recovered after a long break imposed by said health issues, I was able to sing Bach's Mass in B Minor without the slightest fatigue. And that's when my fellow choir-mates noticed my renewed voice and, consequently, my entirely new charisma.

Luckily not everyone aiming to achieve personal development and a freer voice has such an arduous path before them, but everyone does have to take that first step. Since you're holding this book, congratulations, you already have. My greatest hope for this humble little volume is that it will inspire you and pave the way to a plethora of richly resonant experiences yet to come.

Vocal development as a path to personal harmony

Our voice is an important part of our personality. The sound of our voice expresses who and how we are, as well as the tune and tenor of our mood, even more clearly and immediately than our words do. Many of us only become aware of our voice when we have problems with it: when we feel a lump rise in our throat during an intense conversation or an important presentation; when we're so excited we can't speak or our voice cracks with emotion; when we sound squeaky in situations where we want to be taken seriously; when we aren't heard or have no voice, be it literally or figuratively.

Our voice is an important means of expression. We mostly communicate vocally with our fellow humans, so the voice is a key tool for self-expression, the exchange of ideas, and for understanding. Craftspeople are always mindful of their tools; they take good care to sharpen them, hone them, and keep them in good shape. Such maintenance makes their job easier. Similarly, when we treat our voice (and all that accompanies it) with care, we can express what we feel, think, and want to convey in a more nuanced way. We can develop our voice just as we can promote our sense of self, our physical agility, and our mental strength.

With this book, I in no way aim to burden you with any (additional) tasks for your everyday life. Instead, I simply invite you to become more aware of your voice—to lovingly use it during a few minutes of spare time each day, and playfully explore its possibilities. You'll soon find your voice growing livelier, more sustainable, and more resilient. All this will also help you develop your own distinctive voice that, in turn, will have a positive effect on your mood, your ability to communicate, your goals for personal development, and your physical well-being. Naturally, by extension, these improvements will also have positive effects on your relationships with others.

The many little exercises that follow will help in these endeavors. As you read, keep the emphasis on *little* in mind. Our guiding principle: Just five minutes every day—at home or during a brief break at the office—is preferable to an hour only once a week.

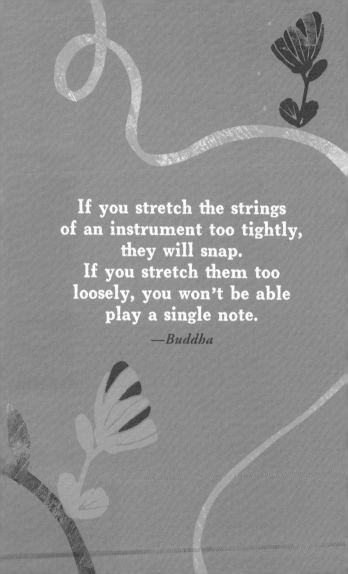

If you stretch the strings
of an instrument too tightly,
they will snap.
If you stretch them too
loosely, you won't be able
play a single note.

—*Buddha*

1
Your Body
as Musical
Instrument

What do you and a cello have in common?

A musical instrument's ability to sound good depends on how it vibrates. The same is true of the human body. Our bones transmit sound and our tissues resonate, too, unless they're blocked. Our voice isn't limited to our larynx and vocal cords; it's a whole-body phenomenon. Try putting your hands on your sternum and, next time you exhale, say "Aaah." Do you feel the sound vibrating under your hands?

The body of a cello also looks a lot like the human body—after all, whether we call one a "resonance box" or "sound board," they're both bodies. The cello is a fascinating instrument with a rich variety of sound. You, too, have everything you need to produce a rich voice. When your body is open, supple, flexible, and you're in a fairly good mood—not too tense, not too tired—it is an ideal resonance box for your voice.

Tune your instrument

In this chapter, I invite you to consider your whole body as an instrument capable of giving your voice space and making your words resound. This will eventually lead you to find harmony between your body and your mood. Sound is vibration, and vibration is movement. We'll see what this means as we get moving: we'll sound good and feel well tuned.

Movement—whether physical sports or mental exercise—helps us become one with our bodies. Most sports encourage good circulation, metabolism, and muscle tone, and require breathing, flexibility, coordination, strength, and stamina—all of which are the foundation of a healthy voice. You've probably already experienced for yourself how physical exercise makes you feel good and boosts your mood. Since few of us have an hour each day for sports, yoga, or relaxation, I'll share a few exercises you can easily incorporate into everyday life here and there, five minutes at a time. Even when they don't directly involve your voice, these exercises will have a positive effect on it. Once you develop a good physical foundation, plus healthy movement and posture patterns you will speak better without even having to think about it.

Get in gear!

Sometimes we hear this phrase when inertia gets the best of us, or we're figuratively stuck and can't move forward. But let's take it literally, as an invitation to get moving, and make it a motto in our everyday life! Taking every opportunity to walk or move, whenever and wherever, will boost your mood and lift your spirit. Thanks to a bit of physical activity, you'll find that other areas of life come into motion, too. "Move a muscle, change a thought": this maxim applies to brainstorming, problem solving, professional progress, and dealing with our fellow human beings.

Whether it's riding a bike to work, going for a walk, or taking the stairs instead of the elevator, even a tiny bit of exercise is good for your whole body and therefore also good for your voice.

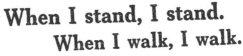

When I stand, I stand.
When I walk, I walk.
—from a Zen story

Good to your feet = light on your feet

If we want to make strides in everyday life and the long term, we'd best pay attention to our feet. Good, sure footing grounds us, laying the foundation for a healthy voice, and is important for our ability to take a stand, both literally and figuratively.

Whether you get a foot massage, roll a small ball under your bare foot while seated at your desk, or take the time to practice standing with good posture, all of this will help you feel better in body, voice, and mind.

Walk barefoot

Whenever possible, go barefoot: If you have a backyard, after getting up in the morning go for a barefoot stroll through the dewy grass or in the snow; do the same during your lunch break, and whenever you have some free time—for instance, on weekends and on vacation. It grounds you and has a beneficial effect on the whole body thanks to the many zones of sensation in the soles of your feet. To feel these zones plus the ground's various textures, roll on your soles—from heel to arch to toe—bringing attention to your feet every step of the way.

There are musicians and singers who perform barefoot, precisely because it helps them connect even better with the space around them and its unique vibrations. A famous example is the virtuoso Scottish solo percussionist Evelyn Glennie. Almost entirely deaf since childhood, she *feels* sounds using her whole body—above all, through the contact between her feet and the ground.

Get swinging

Dangling and swinging motions have many positive effects: they open up our joints and make them more flexible, they stimulate good circulation and help boost rhythmic breathing, and they relax and tone our muscles. The following short exercises will help set you swinging and will activate your body and mind with good vibrations.

Rag doll and ringing bell

Stand with your legs apart, knees slightly bent and flexible. Bring your chin to your chest and slowly roll downward, from your neck to your waist, one vertebra at a time, until your upper body and arms are hanging near the floor. Just relax here for a few breaths and enjoy dangling like a rag doll. Then start swinging your upper body and arms like a pendulum—to the left, middle, right, and back again—steadily, like a swinging bell. Keep your knees elastic and your feet solidly rooted to the ground. Savor this swing, then let it gradually come to an end. Keep breathing and, starting with your lumbar vertebrae (in your lower back), slowly roll back up, unfurling the spine again, one vertebra at a time. Last, lift your head. In addition to loosening your body, this exercise also increases blood flow to the brain. Newly refreshed, you can now concentrate on getting back to work.

Leg swings

Stand upright with your right foot propped up on top of a step, or a sturdy footstool, or something similar. Use your right hand to brace yourself against a wall or the back of a chair. Now swing your free-hanging left leg back and forth. Do this for a few minutes, paying close attention to how the motion feels. Enjoy its effect on your body and breathing. Then switch sides and swing the other leg. This exercise relaxes and refreshes your legs, loosens your hip joints, and keeps your body mobile.

Hand fans

Fan your hands horizontally, as if you've just washed them and have to shake the water off. Feel the momentum spread from your wrist to your fingers and back up your whole arm, and relish the sensation. This little exercise relaxes your arms, hands, and wrists. By loosening your wrist joints, it also has a positive effect on your breathing.

"Dancing Queen"

You probably know this song by ABBA, or at least the title—it's the epitome of someone completely letting themselves go, dancing and devoting everything to the music and its movement. You don't have to hit a club to have this kind of experience, nor do you have to listen to disco. Put on some music of your choice: an upbeat, hard-rocking tune if you want to work out, something softer to help you relax and wind down, or both, back-to-back. Close your eyes, if possible (not while driving!), and let the sound and rhythm lead you. It's not about specific dance moves—just have fun experimenting. Start with your hands, for example, and then let the movement spread through your arms, upper body, and so on. Take advantage of the fact that your body has so many moving parts, and play around. By the time the music is over you'll be refreshed with a renewed degree of concentration and elated to return to your daily or after-work routine.

Learn to dance, dear, lest the angels in heaven not know what to do with you.

—*Saint Augustine*

Sound body, sound mind

Our mental, psychological, and physical selves are deeply connected. When our body is in balance, our mind and mood are, too, and everything feels safe and sound. If, on the other hand, we're out of balance or "beside ourselves" with any kind of negative emotion, it's important that we find our way back—to center ourselves and reestablish balance in our lives. Our language has many idioms and images for this intertwining of body, mind, and soul. We'll make the most of these connections in the following exercises, beginning with the body, experiencing how it affects the mind and psyche. Just as sailors use a sounding line—a rope with distance markers—to "sound out" the sea's depth, we can sound our own depths to achieve a sound body and mind. Being in balance can also be expressed as being in harmony. When we're solid on our feet, things have a way of sorting themselves out for the best.

Plumb line, all's fine

Stand upright, feet about hip-width apart, knees flexible. Let your arms hang down beside your torso. Imagine a plumb line passing straight through your body from the crown of your head to the ground between your feet. Begin turning side to side, keeping your whole body soft and flexible, making small circles around the plumb line. Then shift to trace figure eights with your pelvis—the figure eights' midpoint will center on your same plumb line. Let your breath flow as smoothly as possible. This movement doesn't need to be a grand gesture—a simple version of this can even be done while waiting in a checkout line or at a bus stop.

Regal bearing

Stand up straight and, circumstances permitting, close your eyes for a moment. Imagine you're a king or queen with a crown on your head and a magnificent mantle over your shoulders. Feel the powerful significance of your position. Do you feel yourself standing taller, both inside and out? Let your breath flow freely. Now stroll around the room, eyes open, with that same dignified attitude. You might not be a king or queen as in fairy tales or the few countries that still have monarchies, but you are the sovereign of your own life. Use this exercise over and over, whenever you need a gentle reminder of that!

Tightrope walker

Balancing requires and reinforces our ability to stand up straight, concentrate, stay toned, and be centered and at rest. Coordination and balance exercises also strengthen our intercostals—those often-overlooked muscles between our ribs—which, in turn, play an important role in breathing and supporting our voice. Use anything and everything you need to practice balancing: a fallen tree trunk beside the path on your walk in the woods, a boundary line on the soccer field of your local park, the lines between sidewalk slabs, the curb, a rope lying on the ground. Take a look at children's games or think back to how you yourself might've played on a pretend tightrope as a kid. You can also buy special balancing disks and rocker boards for use at home or in the office for short exercise sessions.

Water carrier

I've had a big picture hanging over my piano for several years now, and it still moves me every time I see it. It shows a group of Indian women carrying filled water jugs home atop their heads. They're wearing colorful robes, and many hooped bangles adorn their arms. They carry their heavy burdens with such grace, dignity, and admirable posture that I marvel at the image every day as if I'd never seen it before. It seems to ask: How do we go through our daily lives? How do we deal with our burdens, our trials, and tribulations? Do we endure them with strength, grace, and dignity, standing upright? Even if the going gets rough, try rising to the challenge: Go through your everyday life like these water carriers. Experience how your body posture affects your inner (and outer!) attitude as well as your outer (and inner!) voice.

2 Breath as the Source of Life

Breath of life, spirit of life

In the Old Testament creation story, God shapes a man from a lump of clay, but this new creature only becomes fully alive when God "breathes life" into him with his own "divine breath"—or should I say, "divine inspiration"? Many languages reflect this connection, and the use of terms like inspire and expire are similarly rooted (in Latin) to the concepts of the soul/spirit entering or leaving the body, respectively. This marvelous creation image conveys and combines everything we experience when we let our breath flow: Our breath connects body and soul; it's what makes us alive. It also echoes our own birth: Our first breath—and, usually, our first cry soon after—marks the beginning of our personal journey through this world.

> # The first thing we must learn is to breathe.
>
> —*Buddha*

Let your breath flow

Of all our bodily functions, breathing enjoys a special status. On the one hand, it is controlled by the autonomic nervous system, so it happens involuntarily; on the other, we can influence it at will. Respiratory training courses and yoga schools use this consciously controlled approach to teach special breathing techniques.

From the moment we're born, the breathing process unfolds in such a way that it literally brings us to life and keeps us alive without our intervention. Over time, physical restrictions and, above all, psychological experiences influence this finely tuned system—but luckily we can also learn how to allow this life-giving breath back again when it shifts out of sync. This requires that we turn our attention to our personal breathing, which—with the help of mindful body and voice exercises—can then be liberated again. Free-flowing breath provides the vital oxygen we need to feel alive, and also gives a greater lightness to the body, mind, and soul. The following exercises will help you (re)discover the gift we each received the day we were born—a natural talent we need only refresh to enjoy anew.

Invite your breath in, and give it a warm welcome

The first step is to get acquainted with your breathing, just as you would with a person you want to get to know a bit better, and maybe even become friends with. The guidelines for building interpersonal relationships also apply to how we handle our breath: Take every opportunity to get to know each other, free of all expectation, and stay open to whatever might develop. The following exercises will allow you to encounter your breath—and, with it, yourself.

Loll about and stretch like a cat

Take pleasure in stretching, lolling, and rolling around—not just in the morning, but multiple times throughout the day. This is beneficial after spending long periods seated at a desk, on a long drive, and so on. Stretching is good for tense muscles as it makes them more mobile again and ensures better blood circulation. It also widens your rib cage, creating more room for deeper inhalation. Feel free to yawn, sigh, and even moan. At home you can crawl on all fours and imitate a cat's movements. It might sound silly, but you'll feel the difference afterward!

Clean your room

Using your tongue, give your entire oral cavity a good "scrub." Run your tongue along the inner and outer sides of your teeth, inside your cheeks and lips,

and across your palate. Keep your lower jaw soft and slightly open, your lips lightly closed and relaxed. After giving the room that is your mouth a thorough clean, let your tongue lie on the floor and rest. Close your eyes and feel a fresh sense of relaxation each time you release your breath. A relaxed tongue not only has a positive effect on your breathing, but also on the throat muscles and their ability to free your voice.

Get in flow

When our breath flows freely, so do our lives. Just as respiratory and other physical blockages can be broken through, so, too, can mental blocks and other areas of life where we might feel stuck be released and eventually return to a flow state. This doesn't usually happen at the flip of a switch. But if we regularly engage in a mindful breathing practice, free of any and all expectations, we'll be better prepared for impasses and will be able to ease ourselves into a more harmonious life.

Loosen your lower jaw

Everyday life often leads us to clench our teeth, and most of the time we don't even notice it. Start paying attention to this every now and then, and consciously loosen your lower jaw while keeping your lips closed. At first it might help to gently place your hands on your cheeks and mandible joints in order to release them. With practice you'll find that you'll be able to do it without your hands. Relaxing our temporomandibular joints—the ones by your ears that connect your jaw to your skull—helps our breath flow better and opens up the throat.

Let your breath ebb and flow

Relax your lips, and as you start to exhale, make an "f" sound—for *free, fluid, focused*—allowing the breath to smoothly flow out. Then wait for the following inhalation to flow in naturally, on its own, and again exhale with an "f" sound. You can even use your hands or index fingers to make "conducting" gestures in the air as you exhale, if it helps you breathe out more smoothly. The most important thing is to focus on the exhalation; let the inhalation happen all by itself. This exercise will lengthen and deepen your breath. It also provides a strong foundation for your voice, which can then carry farther by this free-flowing breath.

Circle your own center

Sit upright in a chair, almost on the edge of the seat. Set your feet and knees hip-width apart and rest your hands on your thighs. Now circle your pelvis

> As long as I breathe, I hope.
> As long as I hope, I love.
> As long as I love, I live.
>
> —*Cicero*

around your "sitz" bones (more formally known as the *ischial tuberosities,* these are the parts of the pelvis you can feel when you sit on your hands). Let your upper body and head be carried along by this movement. Feel how your breathing syncs to the flowing rhythm of this circling motion. After a few rounds, switch to the opposite direction. The circle can be big, small, or anywhere in between—on any given day, your body will tell you what's best.

A reed in the breeze

Stand upright with your feet hip-width apart and in solid contact with the ground. Keep your knees soft and slightly bent. Close your eyes. Begin gently rocking back and forth, as if you were a reed or blade of grass being caressed by the wind. Feel how your body becomes more flexible, especially in the legs, pelvis, spine, shoulders, arms, and neck—and even your head. Is your face relaxed, your lower jaw comfortably loose? Can your breathing relax, too? Don't force it—just let it happen. You can adapt this exercise to be done almost anywhere, even while waiting in line, just keep your eyes open and do very small, subtle movements.

Listen to your breath

Pause every once in a while and turn your attention to the breath. Just observe it, without any judgment. Is your breathing even? Shallow? Are you unconsciously holding your breath? Where do you feel each breath causing movement in your body? Where does it want to go, and where might you be holding it back? Don't try to force any specific kind of breathing. Merely giving it some love and attention can trigger a natural sigh of relief. The first step is to become aware of the breathing process—then connect with it, over and over. You might try this when you're sitting on the couch at the end of the day, waiting in the line at the supermarket, or in the car as you sit at a red light. Just let the breath happen.

Breath as a bowl

Sit upright, square atop your sitz bones, without leaning against the back of the chair and preferably toward the front edge. Set your knees and feet hip-width apart, and hands on your thighs. Gently tilt your pelvis backward as you inhale; your back will be a bit rounded and your chin will sink toward your chest. Then gradually tilt your pelvis forward as you exhale; your back and head will straighten up.

As you do these movements, always rock slowly and consciously over your sitz bones. Imagine that your pelvis is a bowl: As you tip backward, inhaling, your breath flows into your pelvis and rounded back. As you tip forward or sit up straight, exhaling, your breath flows out again—preferably through soft lips shaped to make an "f" sound. Move with the breath. When you've straightened up and fully exhaled, wait for the inhale to return on its own, and then just let it flow into your "bowl." Notice how, between the movement and the breathing, a steady rhythm develops.

Gift yourself a smile

Sit up straight, your feet hip-width apart and well rooted to the ground, your knees equally spaced, and hands on your thighs. Now simply close your eyes and smile. This smile not only shapes your mouth, but extends across your whole face, up to your relaxed eyes and forehead. Can you feel where it's working? Do you notice how it has a relaxing effect on your breathing? Let your attention linger on the breath and its related sensations. Turning inward this way, once a day for a couple of minutes, will give you a greater sense of serenity and well-being.

BREATHE OUT

Be here
Relax
Expand
Accept
Tune in
Hear
Exhale

Open
Unwind
Trust

All creation has a song within
and each song dreams
its own bird.
The world will begin
to sing akin,
all you need is the magic word.

—*Joseph von Eichendorff*

3 Developing Your Voice Through Song and Sound

Using the voice to express and communicate

From the moment we're born, our voice is a means of communication. Without it, our ancestors wouldn't have survived primeval times, and even today it remains our most elementary way of expressing ourselves. Babies whimper when they want food and affection; if their needs aren't immediately met, their whimpers turn into cries, which usually get someone to come and provide whatever they lack. From the very beginning, we communicate even without language, using vocal yet nonverbal sounds. Even later in life, the way we vocalize things—and our voices themselves—plays a large part in how we express ourselves and are understood by others.

Voice and well-being

As we grow from babies to toddlers our vocal development reaches new, more nuanced levels. This becomes evident if you secretly listen in on babies: they'll start babbling to themselves. It gives them pleasure and is good for their health. On the one hand, it stimulates their lips, which are packed with nerve endings; on the other, these vocal sounds and vibrations soothe their small bodies. Over time, more varied vocal sounds are added.

When we watch adults communicating with babies, we see how attuned they are to these vocalizations: most adults start babbling, chuckling, and using much more melodic speech than they would in conversation with other adults. We'll make the most of these observations and insights in this chapter to help our voices resonate and make our vocal expressions more diverse and vivid. We did this as babies without even trying—now it's time to tune back into those same vibes.

Humming, intoning, and rhapsodizing

Humming comforts the body. It deepens and lengthens our breathing, and the resonance and vibrations it creates are like a little body massage from within. A relaxed hum can also help us identify our authentic voice, or so-called *neutral pitch*. Pronouncing vowels, in particular, creates and fills space. The vibrations of these sounds spread throughout our body as well as the space surrounding us. Interestingly, sound, vibration, and spirituality have always been closely associated. It's no coincidence that humming, rhapsodizing, and other types of singing have long held an important place in various spiritual traditions.

Sweet anticipation

Imagine a delicious meal. What does it smell like? What does it look like? How will it taste? Hold that thought, and let an anticipatory "Mmm" rise from your throat, and then another. . . . Can you hear and feel real excitement in both your body and the tone of your voice?

Mmm

Whistle while you work

Oftentimes when we're totally absorbed in the moment, happily busy with some task or in a flow state at work, we spontaneously start to hum. Usually these little ditties arise unconsciously and in a totally relaxed voice. But we don't always have to leave it to chance: You can consciously decide to launch into a light little hum. Experiment, play around with it, and take note of how it feels—as always, with no expectation or judgment whatsoever.

Monotone humming

This humming variant can be practiced on its own or in conjunction with the **ebb and flow** exercise from the previous chapter (p. 20). Once you've exhaled a few times while making that relaxed "f" sound, let your next out-breath give rise to a hum: "Mmmmmmm." Let your lips relax and lightly close, but leave your jaw slightly open. Allow the pitch to emerge on its own, and the tone to determine itself. Then let your next in-breath come by itself. Afterward, if you feel like it, try a few other pitches. Feel its effect—on your breathing, your body, and your mood.

Buzz like a bug

The buzzing "z" sound, when sustained out loud, can best be compared to the sound bees and other flying bugs make. Imagine a bumblebee flying around you, and use your index finger to trace its trajectory. The curves and loops are not just visible in the air, they're also audible. This exercise activates your diaphragm, enlivening both body and voice alike.

A, e, i, o, u

Intoning is a way of exhaling with sound. After practicing a few steady exhalations using the afore-mentioned "f" sound, next time you exhale instead produce any vowel sound you'd like, keeping a consistent tone. When the exhalation and sound come to an end, wait for your next inhalation to come, all on its own, and then intone the vowel again as you exhale. Stay with this vowel for a few breaths. If you'd like, try out a few different pitches. With the next inhalation, just think of the vowel. How does the vowel sound affect you? Where do you feel its vibration in your body? Practice using a different vowel. Where and how does this one affect you?

Sound painting

Just as we can visually paint with colors, we can also aurally "paint" with sounds. The best example is with onomatopoeia. We use the Greek term *onomatopoeia*, which means "name I make," for words that phonetically imitate or suggest the sounds they describe. This phenomenon extends into the visual realm, capturing the connection between color and sound. Just as we speak of perceiving *colors' tones* in the visual realm, we similarly distinguish between *tones' colors* in the audible realm—it's no coincidence that we talk about *blues music* or opera singers' *coloratura*, literally their "coloring" of an aria. In many onomatopoetic words, and even entire poems, the sound of speech clarifies its content. Try it for yourself: *hisssss, whooooosh, blah-blah-blah,* babbling on. . . . Our languages and voices aren't mere sounds and modes of communication, but—as we've already seen—they're also physical experiences. Try tasting language, letting it melt in your mouth.

Savor the syllables

Consonants stimulate our body. They engage our diaphragm and other parts of the body involved in creating speech—lips, tongue, palate—and also help carry the sound of our voice to the outside world. Relish each consonant as you speak. Let such syllables burst like balloons, fizz like firecrackers, tickle your tongue, lilt off your lips. . . .

Play ball

Dribble an imaginary ball in front of you, alternating hands with each bounce, and make the following sounds: *p-p-p, t-t-t, k-k-k*. Apply the same springlike momentum of the hands' movement to each individual consonant. Most important, release all tension in your hands, lower jaw, and everywhere in your body after every movement so that the air you inhale before the next gesture will come automatically each time. It might seem like a small detail, but it's enough to make a big impact.

Let the sounds resound

Some *sonorant consonants* (those with a continuous sound) and *obstruents* (those with obstructed airflow)—in linguistic terms—require not only our lips, tongue, and palate, but simultaneously make use of our larynx. Sonorants include *m, n, ng, l, r, y,* and *w*; obstruents include most other consonants, such as the voiced (or buzzing) *z,* popping *p,* and the familiar *f.* Play with words that contain these sounds, speaking slowly and savoring every second. Make sure your lower jaw is loose and you aren't exerting too much pressure. This allows the vibration to spread through your body so that your voice resonates. You can also use these consonants for vocal exercises: make audible sighs and rising or falling tones without adding vocal pressure.

Peter Piper

Throughout childhood, tongue twisters thrilled many of us. We inevitably floundered about and muddled our words at first, so training can be not just fun and effective, but downright hilarious. Rifle through your memories and give the old phrases a go. Here are some examples to get you started:

Peter Piper picked a peck of
pickled peppers,
a peck of pickled peppers
Peter Piper picked.

Betty Botter bought some butter,
but, she said, the butter's bitter;
if I buy better butter, it will make
my batter better.

A skunk sat on a stump and thunk the
stump stunk, but the stump thunk the
skunk stunk.

How much wood would a woodchuck
chuck if a woodchuck could chuck wood?

Cork dork

Speaking with a cork between your front teeth is an excellent way to practice articulation. It might make you feel like a dork, but it's also an ideal reason to enjoy a bottle of wine with your loved ones—solely to get a good cork, of course. If you don't have a cork on hand, your finger can also work: just lightly pinch your thumb and forefinger together and place them between your teeth. Try saying or reading a short text out loud—a snippet from the newspaper, say, or even a poem—and make it as clear and comprehensible as possible despite your new oral obstacle. Then remove the cork or fingers, and say it again. Hear how wonderfully clear your enunciation is now?!

Story time—out loud!

Read aloud from time to time, alone or in company, and enjoy being creative and expressive with your voice.

The color of song

Singing is vibration. Picture sound waves, just like the wavelengths of different types of light. Colors, too, are vibrations of sorts. And so, singing makes life vibrant: vibrant color, colorful sound vibrations. It's not just about the tones' colors, it's about the big and small vibrations that singing creates within our bodies and psyches—the kind of vibes that can bring us into harmony with ourselves and others. Singing is the opposite of life's quiet, unsung acts. Singing connects us. Singing comforts us. Singing makes us happy. Singing frees us. Singing enchants us. . . . Try it and see—*feel*—for yourself!

Singing for health

Recent neurobiological and music-therapy research has confirmed much of what we've intuitively felt and experienced for thousands of years while singing. Singing reduces fear and aggression. It helps reduce stress and strengthens the immune system. It creates positive forms of attachment, can lighten depressive states, and can even relieve pain. It increases our satisfaction with life, as well as our sense of self-efficacy. It has been scientifically proven that singing releases hormones related to happiness and inhibits hormones related to stress. Likewise, breathing and other rhythmic corporeal practices help balance and harmonize our minds by forming new synapses in the brain. Singing promotes our physical, mental, and spiritual health in so many ways—and is completely free of any harmful side effects.

Singing with heart and soul

To do something with body and soul means to be completely absorbed or, as some might say, in a flow state, and when this is the case, we find ourselves living fully in the moment. The mental treadmill on which so many of us often find ourselves mindlessly sprinting, consumed by worries about past and future, stands still. When we sing, we're fully immersed—whether singing solo or with others. Afterward we resurface feeling refreshed.

Try singing as you tend to everyday tasks like housework, your commute, or your morning or evening stroll. Everything goes better with a song, because singing makes us happy!

4

On Hearing and Listening In

Our ears are the gates through which the world enters our inner being, and our voice is the bridge from our inner life out into the world and to our fellow people. These two portals belong together, and they're the paths through which we build relationships.

The development of our voice is inseparable from our hearing. The ear and the auditory nerves are formed very early in the gestational period; an unborn child can already hear by the middle of a woman's pregnancy. Around the same time the fetus also starts distinguishing sounds and reacting to

> **Remember the voice
> deep within you!
> It's to be treasured, like life,
> through and through.**
>
> —*Matthias Claudius*

them, and the mother's voice is deeply imprinted.

By adulthood—even though our sense of hearing has long since been established, physiologically speaking—we can, to a certain extent, refine and develop it. We can hone our capacity for hearing and listening, which has everything to do with paying attention, focusing, being mindful, and being dedicated. The phrase *to be all ears* paints an apt picture, and speaks volumes about our ultimate aim.

This chapter contains a few suggestions, inspirations, and interesting facts about hearing and listening. By becoming more sensitive to your sense of hearing, you'll soon discover that it's about so much more than merely processing

sound waves in the brain. Once our aural perception is refined, we become more attentive to life's subtler nuances. This, in turn, positively affects our ability to communicate.

Voices and sounds all around

Put your antennas out there every now and then: Listen attentively and sensitize your ears to the voices in your environment, including your own. Analyze and reflect on your listening experiences. You might be surprised by what you find.

Listen to the voices of others

Most of the time we respond to other people's voices subconsciously. Try listening more carefully: How do certain people speak? What effect do their voices have on you? Why do they have those effects? Why do you like a particular voice, or why not? This type of personal research can be fascinating. Pay attention to how the voices of radio or television personalities affect you. For example, listening to a sampling of female news anchors, I've found that some speak in as deep a voice as possible; it's probably to under-line the seriousness of the news (and their delivery of it)—but, pushed past a certain point, it ceases to sound coherent.

Voices move us

Much like hands, voices can strike us like a slap on the face or can cheer us up, comfort us, caress us, and so much more. They have a similar way of touch-ing us, too, although voices do so through the nerve cells in our ears, whereas hands do so through the nerve endings in our skin. Neuroscientific research is still exploring how others' voices resonate with our own, and vice versa. If a speaker has a husky or rough voice, as listeners, we are tempted to clear our throats. When a speaker talks in a free, relaxed, and lively voice, we also feel relaxed and open as we listen. This explains the magic of certain voices. A well-(re)sounding voice creates a sense of well-being—which can further motivate us to continue developing our own voices.

Tune in to others while staying within yourself

If you're aware of how your own voice is impacted by those around you, you can distance yourself from the potentially unpleasant effects of others' voices—effectively empowering you to protect yourself. So if the sound or tone of someone's voice causes anxiety or unease in your body or mind, try to stay securely within yourself: Focus on your breath and on relaxing your neck, shoulders, and anywhere else tension can develop.

Hear your own voice

How do you perceive your own voice? Most people are surprised and even appalled when they hear a recording of their own voices: "What?! That's what I sound like?" We normally hear ourselves differently, primarily because we can easily confuse how we hear external sounds (like other people's voices) and how we hear internal sounds, because the vibrations are conducted through our own bones and bodily tissues. Befriend your own voice: Record it with your smartphone every now and then and listen to it— you can even read or say the same thing each time. The many exercises and recommendations in this book will gradually make an audible difference.

Listening as lively encounter

Real listening can only happen under certain conditions: You need to be fully present, avoid interrupting your conversers, not prematurely impose your opinions on them, and give them and their concerns adequate space. Don't be afraid to request the same from them in return.

All ears

There are two types of *listening in*. There's the negative type: eavesdropping, which is done with bad intentions. Someone is overheard or eavesdropped on in order for the eavesdropper to snatch a secret and possibly do harm. If, on the other hand, we listen in with good intentions and real dedication to someone telling us something, it's another story entirely. With the positive type of listening in, dialogue can take place with openness, mindfulness, and goodwill. That's when we say we're *all ears*.

Hearing others

If, as just described, we're all ears, then we can truly hear those we're speaking with and perceive their current conditions, mental states, or moods. This happens above all through the sound of their voices—we can hear, feel, and really sense how they're doing, even if their words try to tell us otherwise.

Sea and forest

Who doesn't love hearing the sounds of the sea, a lake's waves gently and steadily lapping the shore, or birds chirping in the forest? If your next vacation is still far off and you can't escape into nature any sooner, then here's another option. Lie on your back, on a soft carpet, and rest your head on a pillow. If it's helpful, cover up with a blanket. Put on a playlist featuring natural sounds of your choice. Let your breath flow calmly, and completely surrender to the sound of the sea, the wind in the trees, a babbling brook, or whatever you prefer on this particular day. This, too, is a type of lively encounter: it helps you focus on your relationship with yourself through sound.

The blessing of silence

It isn't easy to find silence these days, but it is still possible. It can be even more difficult to become and remain quiet at your very core. For most of us, this requires practice. Our days are often chock-full, from dawn to dusk—and very few of us begin or end each day with a long meditation. Practice sitting still in silence, starting out with just a few minutes each day. This will instill the initial discipline, and help ease you into your day. See how it goes—should this spark a desire in you to spend more time in calming silence, go ahead and lengthen each session in tiny increments, since meditating on the absence of sound helps sharpen our ability to tune in over time.

> **Let the water settle;**
> **you will see moon and stars**
> **mirrored in your being.**
> —*Rumi*

Our ears are always on

We can close our eyes when they're exhausted, but our ears are always "on," even as we sleep. To some extent, our brain filters incoming audio: When we're deeply focused on one thing, we often unconsciously block out other sounds. Or we subconsciously practice selective hearing: A sleeping mother won't usually be woken up by noises on the street, but she will hear and be roused from sleep when her baby becomes restless. Despite such innate filters, we must still take good care of our hearing and shield our ears from harm.

Protect your hearing

There's hardly any silence left in our everyday lives—every which way we turn, we're bombarded by noise, whether it's passing cars, loud construction sites, or blasting music. Make as much room as possible for peace and quiet in your personal and professional spheres. It will do you and your ears a world of good.

The sound of silence

Search for the silence wherever and whenever you can, even in the tiniest nooks and crannies of your everyday life. Take a few minutes in the morning or in between tasks at work to just silently look out the window, take in a picture, or admire a flower. Is there a park on your way to or from work that's inviting you to pause and enjoy just ten minutes of peace and quiet? Accept the invitation and take every such opportunity. Focus on your breath without trying to influence it in any way.

The greatest revelation is silence.

—*Lao Tzu*

Your inner voice

Listening and living with attentiveness makes us more sensitive beings, which also makes us better able to perceive our own inner voice. Some call it *intuition*. Others see it in the visions that arise each night in their dreams. Still others actually hear words and sentences formulated in an unidentifiable place deep within, and refer to it as the *voice of the heart*.

Listening In

When birds and clouds fly with ease,
windmills turn with earth's orbit,
when reeds bend with the breeze,
then listen in and be quiet.

Listen to the sun when it sets each evening,
and when it wakes the flowers each morning.
Listen to the rain drip gently at the window,
and to the heart that beats within you.

Listen each day to the laughs friends share.
Rejoice over all of life's little things.
And give the gift of a real laugh, and care
for those who take you under their wings.

What's it all mean, you ask?
Just listen in, that's your task.

—*Leonard Ritschel*

5 Well-Tuned All Day, Every Day

As we saw with the musical parallels in earlier chapters, our voices can express whether we're well-tuned, in good spirits, and balanced—or not. The tenor of our voices and how attuned we are to our surroundings and selves are inseparably intertwined aspects of our being. Our voices make audible—to ourselves and our companions—how we feel, the shape we're in, and how (un)balanced we are. Conversely, our voices can also influence our moods: They can lift low spirits, help us tune out all troubles and, like Glenn Miller's popular hit, get us "in the mood."

In this chapter, together we'll go through the course of an average day so you can see how these exercises might best fit into your daily routine.

The early bird gets the . . . word!

The common claim that "the early bird gets the worm" hints at how to get the day off to a successful start—start early! In keeping with the theme of this book, let's expand on it to say that "the early bird gets the *word*." Feel free to laugh as you remember this silly switcheroo each morning—that, too, will help get you in tune for a vocally vibrant, artfully articulate, well-enunciated day!

Wake up your voice

Most of us stretch a bit in the morning upon first getting up—it helps make us more agile after a night's sleep, and also boosts our circulation. If you yawn a lot as you stretch, it helps give your breathing greater momentum, too. Ideally, we'd all have time for a little gymnastics each morning. Anything that does our main muscles good at the start of the day is equally applicable to the many small muscles in our larynx and vocal cords: they, too, need a warm-up each morning to get going. Audibly yawn, sigh, and groan as much as you want before getting up. Then feel free to start humming or making all sorts of sounds, just as we discussed back in chapter three. Remember, no expectations! It doesn't matter how it sounds; the most important thing is that it feels good.

Lather up with a *la-la-la*

Your daily warm-up can continue straight into the shower or, if you're feeling groggy and in need of particular reinforcement, simply start there. Use a joyful "aaah" under a steaming stream of water to then launch into a morning aria—make it up as you go or sing one of your favorite tunes. If you're one of the hardy types who likes to end your shower with a rush of ice-cold water, then sharp exhalations and shocking exclamations should become a key part of the program. Whatever your preferred approach, the goal is to start out not just physically refreshed, but also vocally reinvigorated—and therefore *tuned in* and *tuned up*—for the rest of your day.

Take off with good vibes

Imagine you're an airplane—let's find a way to take off from everyday life. Spread your arms out like wings, and start roaring like an old-school engine, *brbrbrbrbrbrbr*.

Don't use your tongue to roll your *r*'s; instead, purse your lips and exhale powerfully, humming with your throat, so your lips flutter against each other as you breathe out. This "lippy" *r* will make it easier for your voice to imitate an airplane as it swoops through the air, making ups and downs, loop the loops, and hitting new heights. This is a great way to get your voice up and going each day. It also literally creates "good vibrations": the flutter of your lips and the buzz from your throat form sound waves that permeate the entire body, waking it up while simultaneously soothing it. Good vibes for the body are good vibes for the mind—give it a try!

Rise and shine

Why not welcome your fellow human beings to take part in your good morning mood? Awaken your loved ones or greet your neighbors and colleagues with a melodic, lively voice. This might well cause a bit of surprise the first time around. In any case, you'll soon see that it has a more positive effect than a sullen "get up!" or mumbled "g'mornin'." You will help everyone start the day with a spring in their steps.

Readjust throughout the day

The effects of your morning tune-up, not to mention your reserves of vocal and respiratory strength, will last longer if you periodically pause for readjustment. It will help you breeze through the day and even have some leftover energy for a relaxing evening after a productive day's work.

Balance in the interim

How are you feeling right now? Express it vocally whenever circumstances permit. Hiss, moan, groan, sigh. If you're frustrated or angry with someone or something, stick your tongue out when you have a moment to yourself, and accompany the facial expression with a confident "grr," "d'oh," "blah," or "meh." Such vocal expressions help us process aggression and other unpleasant emotions. You'll feel better almost immediately.

If you're feeling good, you can also express that vocally, with an appreciative "mmmh," "aaah," or astonished "oooh," all of which reinforce positive feelings.

Take a break

Breaks are important. Be sure to pause from time to time in the middle of everyday life. Often just a minute or two will suffice. Breaks are also important when it comes to speaking. Punctuation divides written language, but it also helps direct our speech: Don't speak without honoring those periods and commas. At the very least, give yourself space at the end of every sentence to allow time for a full breath before proceeding with the next thought. This tranquil pace is good for you, your voice, and especially your interlocutors—it'll make it much more pleasant for them to listen to whatever you have to say.

Get back in the groove

If by midday you find you haven't spoken for a while, take a moment to briefly tune up again before making any phone calls or going into a meeting. You can just make a light, comfortable humming tone or do one of the other exercises from chapter three. If you've been glued to your desk, sitting for a long time, briefly reactivate your body with some stretching and take a few energizing steps around the office.

On the phone

When on phone calls, sit up as straight as you would in direct conversations. Our exterior posture affects our interior attitude as well as our voice—during a call, these details are audible and perceptible on the other end of the line. If the ringing phone startles you in the middle of work, try to first briefly collect yourself—or at least catch your breath—before picking up.

King Kong

To revitalize your voice and your whole body, pretend you're King Kong: Stand with your legs wide apart, knees slightly bent, and bounce up and down a bit. Lightly clench your fists and gently pummel your torso, thighs, lower back, and behind. Drumming your fists on your chest, make "aaa," "eee," "ooo," and "uuu" sounds. Whether you take it seriously or not, it'll work!

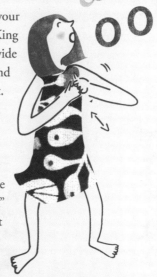

Delight in the little things

Amid the daily grind we tend to let ourselves get wrapped up in so many appointments and commitments that sometimes everything feels like a chore. An excess of obligations as well as the sheer monotony of everyday duties conspire to narrow our field of vision. Pay attention to the little things, experiences, and encounters that can turn an average day into an extraordinary one, whether it's the smile of a stranger on the way to work, a chirping bird outside the window, a coffee break with colleagues, a friendly greeting in the stairway, the first tulip to sprout in springtime, the first snowflake welcoming in winter.

Laughter

Laughter is good—not just for your body and mind, but also for your breath and voice. Everyday life doesn't always give us reason to laugh, but we should nevertheless remain open to the possibility. Laughter's positive effects are strongest when we laugh *at ourselves* and *with others*; needless to say, laughing *at others* doesn't have the same effect. As an interaction between body and psyche, laughter activates the diaphragm and voice, resulting in good moods, feelings of well-being, and happiness.

Amazement

Amazement isn't always associated with a vocal expression, but even when it's silent it has a way of affecting our voice and mood. When we're amazed, we're entirely open and perfectly present. These special states of being are experienced not only on spiritual and emotional levels, but on a physical level as well—their effects are noticeable and even palpable: in our eyes, our facial expressions, our bodies, our breathing, and around our larynx. Astonishment broadens the resonance chambers of our mind. If you go through your day with an inner attitude of gratitude and an ability to marvel at life, it will be audible in your voice. Amazement's magnetic effects can make virtually anyone more charismatic.

Excitement

Give voice to your pleasure. You don't necessarily have to jump for joy or triumphantly cheer—contentedness can be audible when you let yourself go a little and allow it to melodiously buoy the words you say. Do you feel life has given you no cause to rejoice? Oftentimes we let negativity take over, turning everything blasé and gray. Keep an eye out for

even the smallest sources of positivity along your way, even—*especially*—in difficult times. And consciously keep your voice and melodious intonation alive: They can turn even the dullest everyday gray tone—be it visual or aural—into vivid Technicolor.

Thoughts color our moods

Pay attention to your thoughts. Negative thoughts, mental moaning and groaning, distrust, resentment, envy, anger, and hatred are all reflected in the tone of our body, breath, and voice. It goes without saying that such feelings also powerfully influence our mood. It isn't a matter of looking at everything through rose-colored glasses or sticking to only positive thoughts—swallowing or stuffing down your emotions can be painful. If you feel trapped in negative thought loops, you need to find a way to process and express such feelings in a way that won't harm anyone. We've already covered a few of the vocal possibilities, but there's another way: Dump out the flood of thoughts by writing. Just write without thinking about form, phrasing, or style. This relieves and clears the mind. Amazing ideas and constructive solutions will soon emerge with surprising frequency. All these options for self-expression will help you consciously let go of negative thoughts. You might feel battered by crises and problems—but can you find a way to consider them challenges for growth? It'll take some practice, self-discipline, and mindfulness at the beginning, but it's rewarding for your well-being, voice, mood, and inner equilibrium.

Evocative evenings

It's increasingly hard for us to transition from the hustle and bustle of the day into the calm of evening. The age-old natural rhythms—day and night, hours of dark and light, work and after-work free time—are no longer givens for many of us. Lots of us charge full steam ahead right up until we fall into

> # The soul is dyed by its imaginations.
> —*Marcus Aurelius*

bed, utterly exhausted. But our body and soul still need a good transition so we can tune in to the peace and quiet of nighttime and sink down into a truly restful sleep.

Let the day fade

Let the day fade away in the literal sense. If it was especially good, go ahead and let out a "yeah!" Otherwise just bid it farewell with a relaxing "aaah" or "haaa." Accept the day as it was and let it go, mentally and vocally. You can also end the day with a mindful breathing ritual: with a long exhale (saying "f," a sound that'll be an old friend by now), consciously breathe the day out, so to speak; then, inhaling slowly, picture this new breath bringing in the rest and relaxation of nighttime deep into your lungs, into the very core of your being. This works best when sustained over a few calming breaths.

Gratitude

Glance back at the end of the day and consciously collect the positive emotions and experiences, even if they seem ever so small. You might even choose to write them down in a little notebook. This humble little day's-end review, and the occasional flipping back through to reread some of your notes, will permanently change your underlying mood—and consequently the quality of your voice.

> The bell fades away,
> the flowers' scent is ringing—
> early eventide.
> —*Matsuo Basho*

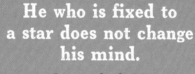

He who is fixed to
a star does not change
his mind.

—*Leonardo da Vinci*

6 Taking the Stage:
Striking the Right Note Under Pressure

All the world's a stage . . .

And every stage is different. Each of us experiences our own stages: public or private, large or small, and we perceive them all subjectively. On some we act quite naturally, whereas others present us with major challenges and opportunities for growth.

Say you're as prepared as can be for a presentation, professional report, or oral exam, but the mere thought of taking the stage makes you panic. This chapter will help you practice ways to handle stage fright, keep your focus, stay grounded in yourself, and use your voice to find your balance in almost any situation. The same tools can be applied to various situations: important conversations in your personal life, phone calls in your professional life, or the toast you hope to give at your daughter's wedding.

Tuning in

If you're tense before a special event, do your best to accept the feelings of unease. To some extent, stage fright can be a positive thing because it provides energy and focuses on a specific situation. As long as you don't let it get the upper hand or start spiraling out, you can use it to your advantage. So try not to push it away, and instead aim to wield it constructively. The following pages will provide a few tips for how to keep your excitement in check. Try them all out and see which are most suitable for you.

B

R

E

A

T

H

flows

Let go of tension

Mental tension settles in the body. Stand up straight, with your feet hip-width apart and your knees soft, not locked. Start with a good long stretch. If you can yawn, that's even better. Next, pat your whole body with your palms: arms, legs, torso, back, buttocks. This releases the tension, wakes you up, and keeps you present. Don't forget your face: gently stroke your chin, cheeks, and forehead, moving from the center outward, and let your breath flow as best you can.

Stay open

Having a physically flexible body helps us achieve free-flowing breath, and both work together to keep us mentally present. Stand up straight, feet hip-width apart, knees slightly bent. Spend at least a minute flexing your ankles and knees, allowing these small movements to work their way through your entire body, while keeping your feet planted on the floor. Then, as you flex again, shift your weight from one foot to the other. The **reed in the breeze** exercise (p. 21) is also ideal for maintaining flexibility and staying mentally centered.

Settle in, stay present

Once again, assume the upright and flexible standing position described above. Start swinging your arms back and forth, so they mirror each other. Keep your knees soft, and feel how your legs, torso, and upper body are swept along by the motion. Swinging your "wings" like this can help you feel at one with your whole body, providing further inspiration for your upcoming performance. Try repeating the **humming** (p. 30), **ebb and flow** (p. 20), and **airplane takeoff** (p. 55) exercises to keep up the momentum, as they're also ideal in such situations.

Amid all the action

In the middle of all life's various acts, it's good to have a few anchors so you can stay connected to yourself and avoid losing yourself. The best and most obvious is the breath. If you've practiced mindful breathing in everyday life, connecting with your breath over and over, you can summon this skill in mere seconds, just before taking the stage, or whenever the situation calls for it.

Find your footing

If you'll be giving your presentation, talk, or public address standing up, make sure you have a solid stance. You're already familiar with it from several of

> **When feeling scattered, pay attention to your breath.**
>
> —*Buddha*

the previous exercises: stand up straight, legs about hip-width apart, feet well connected to the floor, knees and entire body loose and flexible. Any time you feel tension anywhere in the body, try to consciously let go of it. Even walking a few steps while speaking may help it melt away and keep up the momentum of your talk. A solid physical stance puts you in the best position—both literally and figuratively—to convincingly make your point.

Even when sitting, you can stay well connected, firmly rooted, and "take a stand" on solid ground. In this case, you're "standing" on your sitz bones (see chapter 2). Set your feet hip-width apart and firmly planted on the floor. With small, subtle, and almost

invisible movements you can keep yourself flexible in long sessions where you're forced to remain seated. Again, practicing these tiny stress-dissolving motions in everyday life will help you more quickly call them to mind in difficult situations.

Voice, affect, and effect— well said

If you're in harmony with yourself and with what you're saying, then the following tips will provide greater details on how to strike the right note with your audience.

Find your base

Good grounding or contact with the floor provides an important basis—dare I say *stage*?—for your voice. When we're excited, sometimes our voice can go a bit too high or sound a little squeaky. Set your feet solidly on the floor and release all tension from your body. Then your whole body will once again resonate, and your voice will return to its authentic tone and genuine, natural pitch.

Open your mouth

Don't forget—and I mean this literally—to open your mouth while speaking, so that the sound of your voice can emerge unhindered and clearly comprehensible. This doesn't mean you need to assume an exaggerated grimace. By simply opening your mouth, your lower jaw will also automatically relax.

Flex your voice

If you aim to give a vivid presentation, focus on developing a flexible voice. This involves dynamics like volume (quiet to loud), melody (low to high), speed (slow to fast), and how you place accents, emphases, and pauses. Lively speech is good for your voice as well as for general communication: It enlivens both us and our listeners. Furthermore, when our voice and body stay flexible, they don't tire as fast as they do when speaking in monotone, which more quickly leads to muscle fatigue (not to mention boredom).

Charm, courage, calm
Heart
Attitude
Roominess
Intensity
Steadiness
Mindfulness
Awareness

Cooling Down—
Closing Words

Finale: vocal magic

In every chapter of this book the connection between voice, mood, harmony, coherence, and their effects has been made clear. These connections belong to the "ancient wisdom" of our culture as well as other cultures. This form of knowledge is also evident in our vocabulary and idiomatic expressions, as well as in fairy tales and myths.

The Latin word *cantare* can mean "to sing, recite poetry, or sound off"—among other things—but it can also mean "to charm, enchant, or cast a spell on." The connection between voice and magic is probably as old as humanity itself.

In Greek mythology, Orpheus enchants people, gods, and nature with his singing. He even manages to melt the heart of Hades, god of the underworld, and convince him to release his beloved, Eurydice, from the realm of the dead. (The fact that this ploy fails is a story we'll have to save for another day.)

In the fairy tale "Caliph Stork," the main character's ritual recitation of the magic word *mutabor* enables him to transform into an animal and then back into human form. *Mutabor* is a Latin term and means "I will be transformed." Fairy tales aside, I find the countless connections between magic words and transformational powers intriguing and well worth exploring. In "Ali Baba and the Forty Thieves," the magic words "open sesame" grant the protagonist access to the cave and its hidden treasure. Even in our own lives and everyday experiences we see how our voices can open doors, granting us access to our fellow humans' hearts.

Our voices connect our body and soul, and connect us to ourselves and our fellow human beings. Our voices also connect us spiritually to something that exists above and beyond us. Be inspired, be moved, be touched. Let your words, vocabulary, images, idioms, and stories work their magic on you, and make the insights you've gained here an integral part of your daily life. Here's to ever-more harmony!

A word of farewell

We admire people who have a special presence and are naturally drawn to them. We say they have charisma. The Greek word *charisma* originally meant "God-given," or "God's gift." I am convinced that each and every one of us is gifted. Stand by your principles, be your own best friend, and find your gifts and talents. Do not compare yourself to others. You are unique. A good part of your uniqueness is your personal voice. Develop it, alongside your other gifts—do it for your own well-being and for the well-being of everyone you encounter.

Being tuned in and harmonious doesn't necessarily always mean being funny and in a good mood. Life invariably has its ups and downs. If we accept it as it is and respond to it constructively, then we can have authentic experiences and expressions. That's when we and our lives are in harmony.

The key to your personal harmony lies within. Find it and use it. I hope this book helps you on your way.

Sincerely yours,
Jutta Ritschel

Acknowledgments

In its own special way, writing a book is one path to finding harmony. I'd like to thank my agent, Imke Rötger, and my editor, Susanne Haffner, for their unparalleled collaboration and support. Thanks also to Lena Ellermann for her enchanting illustrations, which are so perfectly in tune with the text. Special thanks go to my son Leonard, who so generously provided his poem "Listening In," thereby further adorning these pages. Finally, I would like to express my deepest thanks to Batya Rosenblum, whose gracious collaboration made this English-language edition possible, and to Alta L. Price, for the playfulness and artistry of her translation.

It's not what we experience but how we are emotionally affected by what we experience which determines our fate.

—*Marie von Ebner-Eschenbach*

About the Author

JUTTA RITSCHEL is a music and voice instructor with more than thirty years of experience specializing in breathing and vocalization. She teaches privately, is a lecturer at the University of Augsburg, Germany, and consults on countless workshops and continuing education classes. Her artistic practice includes performing as an ensemble singer and producing musical projects. A trained pianist, she went on to study elementary music education and is a professionally certified breath therapist and educator. Drawing upon the wealth of her long-standing pedagogical and artistic practices, as well as her personal vocal experience, she connects her clients to a plethora of resources, paths to creativity, and a newfound joie de vivre.